Metric Is Here!

About the Book

Just like the man who saw a camel for his first time and said, "There ain't no such animal," Congress in May, 1974, voted down voluntary conversion to the metric system of measurement in the United States.

Most of the world now measures and weighs everything in metric units, which are as easy to understand as the U.S. monetary system of 1, 10, and 100 (cent, dime, and dollar). Though the House of Representatives—as one newspaperman recently wrote—rejected a bill to "pull the American system of weights and measures up into the 19th century," all of us at some time or other do use metrics. And we are using them to an increasing degree. Athletes compete in courses measured in meters. Pharmacists measure prescriptions in metrics. We buy film for our cameras in metric sizes.

We now stand alone with our official acres, bushels, feet, pints, candlepower, and a score of other unrelated measurements. Even Britain, which originated most of our mishmash of measurements, has abandoned them for the metric system. Someday the United States will bound out of the Eighteenth century and "measure up" to the Twentieth century world of measurements.

Metric Is Here!

by William Moore

G. P. Putnam's Sons   New York

Contents

There once was a student named Peter,
Who asked, ''Why use meter and liter?''
But when he found out
He let out a shout,
''Cause meter and liter are neater!''

— Reported in ''Teaching Children to Think Metric,'' *Today's Education,* April, 1973

1.

Meter and Liter are Neater

For more than a hundred years the Congress of the United States has rejected the metric system of weights and measures. On the most recent vote, May 7, 1974, calling for voluntary conversion to the metric system over a ten-year period, the House of Representatives said no.

The irony is that we *do* use the metric system, but only partially. We also use a chaotic mix of various other measurement systems. Yet the classic example of the simplicity of the metric system is our own money: ten cents equals one dime, ten dimes equal one dollar. The metric system applies units of tens and tenths for all measures and dimensions. The metric system also applies to practically all the nations of the world except Sierra Leone, Gambia, the United States, and a few other nations with the same volume of world commerce and influence as Sierra Leone and Gambia.

Talk with someone your age in any European nation, and even if one of you speaks the other's language, he will never understand if you should tell him your height (feet and inches), your weight (pounds and ounces), or anything about the dimensions you live with, such as miles, yards, gallons, inches, candlepower, or—should you own a horse—hands.

Great Britain, the nation that gave us many of our decrepit systems for counting, weighing, and measuring, has itself abandoned most of those measurements for the more workable metric system.

People who dislike change seem to think that inches and miles and pounds were laid down like holy writ in the long ago. Actually the Anglo-Saxon systems whereby we weigh ourselves or survey our property grew up as planlessly as weeds. For instance, a mile was 1,000 double steps of Caesar's legions, a pound was the weight of 7,000 grains of wheat, and a yard was the circumference of King Henry I's waist—which, some say, was the same distance as from the tip of his nose to the tip of his extended hand. (If that was true, he must have been a very grotesque-looking man.)

The quaint ways whereby the Anglo-Saxons developed measures led to bewildering arithmetic, involving such things as converting 16 ounces and 12 inches to larger and smaller figures. The metric system is much simpler.

SI are the letters used to indicate the modern metric system. SI stands for Systèmes International d'Unités, or, in English, System of International Units. At the General Conference of Weights and Measures in 1960, the United States and some metric nations moved to refine the SI system by forming an international organization, known as ISO (International Standards Organization). The ISO meets periodically to review and improve metric standards.

8

Gabriel Mouton conceived of a system of measurement based on the length of one minute of arc of a great circle of the earth. But Abbé Mouton's idea did not come to fruition until the French Revolution, which began in 1789. Amid all the chaos of those days nothing was more chaotic than the situation in weights and measures. Nearly every town and almost every occupation had its own and different system of measurement. The rising class of businessmen, called the bourgeoisie, found that the many measurement systems in use made it very difficult for them to expand or even carry on trade and business. Being revolutionaries, the businessmen were well represented in the new French government. To meet their demands, the famous statesman Prince de Talleyrand submitted a plan for the creation of a new and uniform system of measurement.

Five of the most illustrious French mathematicians and scientists guided the work. While the guns of the revolutionaries, antirevolutionaries, and foreign armies boomed around them, they courageously carried out the actual measurement on French soil of one degree of a quadrant. A quadrant is the distance from the equator to a pole. With this knowledge they could compute, they thought, the distance from the equator to the north pole. This distance was then divided into 10,000,000 equal-sized spaces, each of which was called a meter.

The meter was the basis of a new and unified system of measurement. Out of the meter came the liter and the gram. When one-tenth part of a meter was cubed, that cube container held an amount of liquid called a liter. A liter was the basic measure of all liquids. When one-hundredth

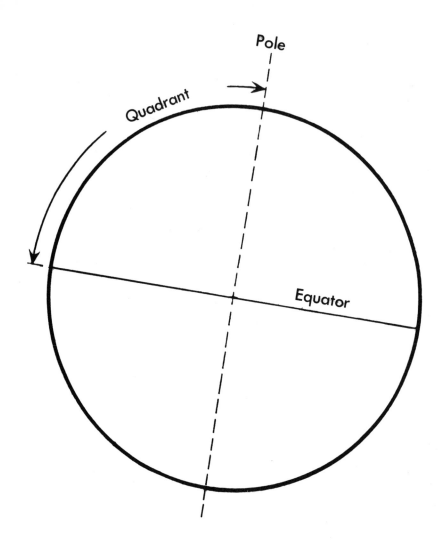

In the late eighteenth century French mathematicians took one quadrant of the earth (the distance from the equator to either pole) and divided it into 10,000,000 equally distant spaces. Each space was called one meter.

of a meter was cubed, that cube container held an amount of water weighing one gram. A gram was the basic measure of weight. Thus the liter and the gram were derived from the meter. In this way measurement of length, liquids, and weight was unified and made understandable.

The scientists made another decision to help bring order out of chaos. The number 10 was made the key to the entire system. The meter was to be multiplied by 10's and divided by 10's. So were the gram and the liter. When ever meter or liter or gram was multiplied by 10, that amount was called a deka. When the deka was multiplied by 10, the amount was called a hecto. When the hecto was multiplied by 10 again, it was called a kilo. Here is the way the metric system was originally constructed:

(Use with Meter, Liter, or Gram)

kilo-	means 1,000
hecto-	means 100
deka-	means 10
deci-	means 0.1
centi-	means 0.01
milli-	means 0.001

As scientists and techniques have become more sophisticated, they have been able to find a standard more exact and universally available than an arc of the earth's circumference. By international agreement in 1960 the meter was redefined in terms of the wavelength of a specific color of light.

Napoleon spread the French metric system throughout continental Europe. After his downfall most of the countries

THE DECIMAL NATURE OF
THE METRIC SYSTEM

	KILOMETER	HECTOMETER	DEKAMETER
KILOMETER	1.	10	100
HECTOMETER	0.1	1	10
DEKAMETER	0.01	0.1	1
METER	0.001	0.01	0.1
DECIMETER	0.0001	0.001	0.01
CENTIMETER	0.00001	0.0001	0.001
MILLIMETER	0.000001	0.00001	0.0001

he conquered retained the system. But Great Britan, mortal enemy of the French and their culture, retained its own complex system of measurements. The fledgling United States, culturally close to Britain and trading chiefly with it, went along with the old British system except for the decimal system of its dollar.

President John Quincy Adams, one of the most brilliant—and unpopular—American Presidents, adored the metric system. But like most of the things that President Adams admired, it was denied by the Congress. Not until 1866 did Congress legalize the metric system for scientists

THE DECIMAL NATURE OF
THE METRIC SYSTEM

METER	DECIMETER	CENTIMETER	MILLIMETER
1000	10,000	100,000	1,000,000
100	1,000	10,000	100,000
10	100	1,000	10,000
1	10	100	1,000
0.1	1	10	100
0.01	0.1	1	10
0.001	0.01	0.1	1

and others who wanted to use it. Few chose to break with familiar ways, however. It would take the forces of commercial competition and almost worldwide use of the metric system to start unofficial change in the United States.

2.

The Switch to Metrics

Louis E. Barbrow, coordinator of metric activities for the National Bureau of Standards in Washington, D.C., picked 1984 as the year when the United States would be predominantly—though not exclusively—metric in its measurement systems.

Barbrow said in mid-1973 that the purpose of legislation pending before Congress "is not to legalize the metric system, but to put planning into the change-over already in progress and make it a matter of national policy." (It was one year later when the legislation came to a vote and the House of Representatives again refused to make the change-over national policy.)

About the same time Barbrow made his forecast, the Ford Motor Company unveiled its first automotive plant in the United States designed to build to metric specifications. Ford's move followed an announcement by the General Motors Corporation that all its new products, components, and facilities, including the rotary engine, would be designed and built to SI specifications.

Change in the system of measurements became necessary

14

in order for the United States to help maintain a favorable international trade position and relate easily to the world community. As aptly stated by Ben Harte in a 1973 article in *The Lamp,* publication of the Exxon Corporation:

> The United States is still trying to export goods defined in feet and inches and pounds and ounces to a world that thinks in terms of meters and kilos. And it not only thinks in those terms but builds, produces and buys and sells in them as well. Trying to fit a four-inch peg into a 10-centimeter hole is becoming increasingly arduous.

Not every industry looked enthusiastically on the switch to SI. Notable was the steel industry, which claimed that the cost of converting the system would not be sufficiently compensated by overseas trade. On the other hand, one of the nation's leading oil companies, Exxon Corporation, said that the changeover to SI would be welcome because all of its ten major European affiliates would be using the metric system by 1975.

Changing to SI still seems inevitable. But it will be costly and complicated and will take many years. There will be two general steps:

1. Changing engineering drawings, labels, road signs, measuring tools, and literally millions of other items to these six basic units of SI:

meter for length
kilogram for mass
second for time

ampere for electric current
kelvin for temperature
candela for light intensity

2. This more difficult and expensive second stage involves redesigning. As only one simple example, this book you are reading was designed and produced in the United States under the old system before the switch to SI. Its pages were measured in inches and fractions of inches. If a British publisher should decide to import its typeset pages, he would have to recompute the page size in SI, the system now used in Britain.

All of us are really more familiar with metrics than we realize. When we ask for 8mm film, 50mg vitamins, or read about a 500-meter race, we are, of course, coping with metric units. We have also met the system in countless radio and television features about science. We cannot escape it, because our country is really an island in a sea of metrics. Slowly, but surely, we have already begun the process of learning to measure the way the remainder of the world measures.

Fortunately for us, the metric method is an easier method to learn than the various English systems we grew up with and struggled to master. It is a unified system. It is unified by the meter and also by the fact that it is based on the number 10 and is therefore decimal. Once you have mastered these two aspects, the rest is easy.

Learning to measure by our old customary methods was made difficult by the fact that we had to learn so many different and unrelated systems. We tried to learn pecks and pints and acres and ounces and all in all a dozen different systems. We also had to cope with some complicated fractions.

Many educators believe that the key to teaching the metric system is to avoid comparing it to inches, pounds, and the like. Wise as this may be for beginning students in a society with a well-established metric system, some comparisons are desirable in a period of transition from one method to another.

Those people who are born after the change becomes official in the United States—if it ever does become official—will have an easier time learning SI than those of us who are already thinking about the change. They will not have to unlearn a few old systems of measurement. Unlearning will be a big problem for many older people if and when the SI does come in to use. Since we know some of the customary ways very well, we want to stick with them simply because they are familiar. For a while we may feel insecure and plaintively ask how many inches are in a meter (all right, if you're insecure, there are 39.37 inches). While it may be useful to make these comparisons occasionally or to have some simple frame of reference, it will be better as soon as possible to forget the old methods and trust the meter. That trust will be rewarded.

3.

The Meter

It may be helpful in the beginning, as a point of departure, to think of the meter as being slightly longer than the yard. Here are a meterstick and a yardstick.

To measure length and common distances it is necessary

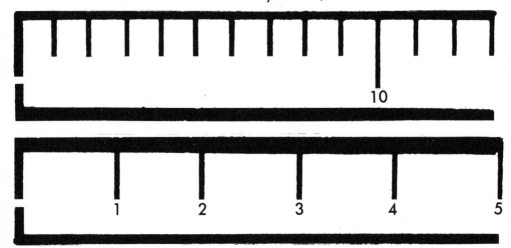

A meter stick and a yardstick are represented above. Below are 13 centimeters of the meter stick and 5 inches of the yardstick, both shown in actual size.

to know only three new metric terms or units. For long distances or anything longer than a meter, use either the meter or the kilometer. Your home, for example, may be only 60 meters from the nearest pizza parlor or, less fortunately, 1,000 meters. If it is 1,000 meters, you can also describe that distance as being one kilometer. It is also perfectly acceptable to say something is one and a half kilometers distance or one and a quarter kilometers distant. Kilo means one thousand. It is a word borrowed from the Greek language; when it appears in the metric system, it represents 1,000. In addition to the word kilometer, you will have to learn centimeter and millimeter.

The centimeter is simply one-hundredth of a meter. The meter is divided into 100 equal-sized spaces, and they are called centimeters. The prefix centi- was borrowed from the Latin language and means one hundred. When written as a number, centi- is written 0.01 and centimeter appears as 0.01m or 1cm. Because SI is based on the number 10 and a decimal system, there are no complicated fractions with which to cope.

For very small distances use the millimeter. The millimeter is one-thousandth of a meter. The meter is divided into 1,000 equal-sized spaces, each of which is called a millimeter. The prefix milli- was also taken from the Latin and means one thousand. Written as a number, milli- appears as 0.001 and millimeter appears as 0.001m or 1mm.

Here is how it looks in table form:

1 kilometer is 1,000 meters
1 centimeter is 0.01 meter
1 millimeter is 0.001 meter

19

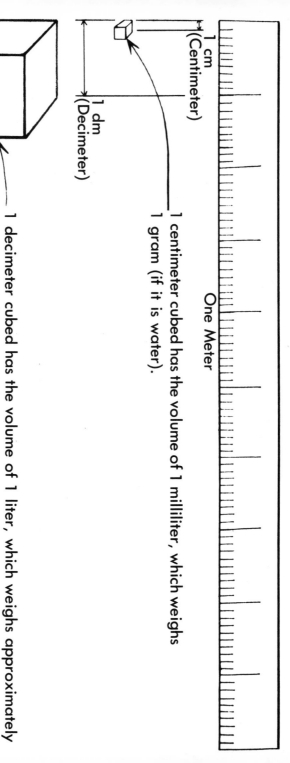

1 cm
(Centimeter)

1 dm
(Decimeter)

One Meter

1 centimeter cubed has the volume of 1 milliliter, which weighs
1 gram (if it is water).

1 decimeter cubed has the volume of 1 liter, which weighs approximately
1 kilogram (if it is water).

For most common measurements of length and distance this is all anyone needs to know. As far as the decimal nature of the system is concerned, it is apparent from this table that the kilo, meaning 1,000, is a multiple of 10. We arrive at 1,000 by multiplying 10 × 10 × 10. Also centi-, meaning 100th, and milli-, meaning 1,000th, are arrived at by dividing with ten. All units in the metric system are arrived at by either multiplying or dividing by 10.

It may help to remember that our money system may also be said to be based on 10. One dollar can be divided into ten dimes and each dime into ten pennies. Ten cents can be written as 0.10¢ and thirty-nine cents as 0.39¢. Correct style in SI also requires that we write whole numbers without the decimal point and quantities less than a whole unit with a decimal point and also a zero before the decimal.

Example: 0.002, not .002.

The mathematicians who created the metric system meant the meter to be the basis of the entire system. The meter was to be multiplied by tens and divided by tens.

They also decided that when one-tenth of a meter was cubed, or when a square container was formed which meas-

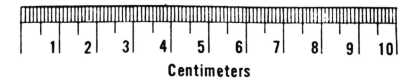

Centimeters

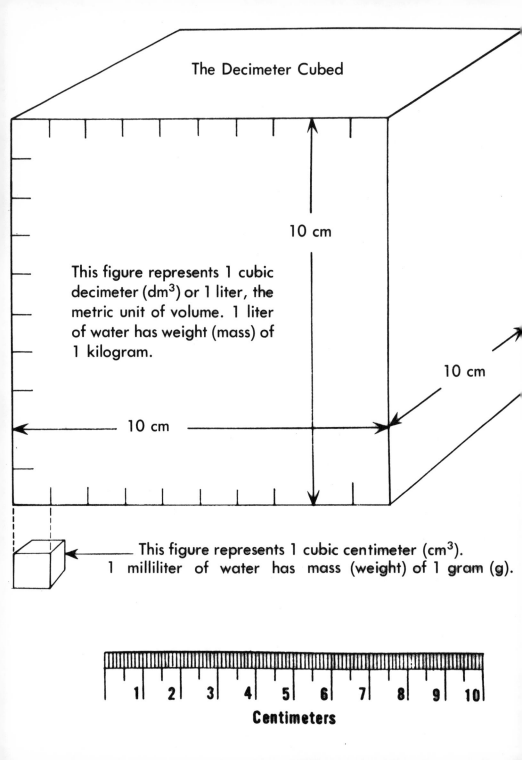

The Decimeter Cubed

This figure represents 1 cubic decimeter (dm^3) or 1 liter, the metric unit of volume. 1 liter of water has weight (mass) of 1 kilogram.

10 cm

10 cm

10 cm

This figure represents 1 cubic centimeter (cm^3).
1 milliliter of water has mass (weight) of 1 gram (g).

1 2 3 4 5 6 7 8 9 10

Centimeters

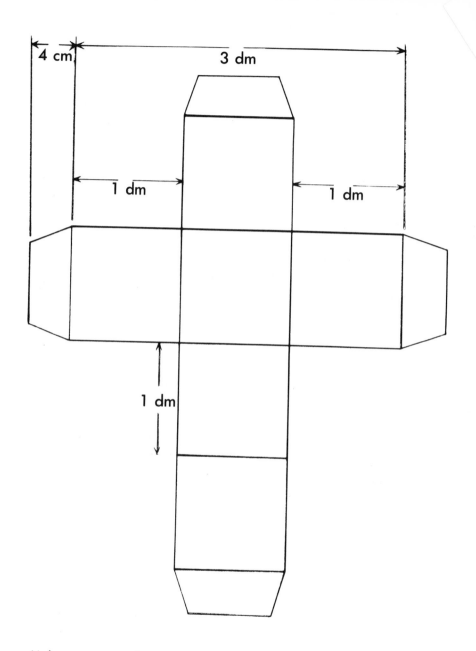

Make your own decimeter cube. Use it to explain the metric system to friends. You need one piece of cardboard 4.8dm by 3.8dm.

ured one-tenth of a meter along all edges, that cube or container would hold an amount of liquid which would be called one liter. The liter was to be the basic unit of measurement of liquids.

They further decided that when one-hundredth of a meter was cubed, or when a square container was formed which measured one-hundredth of a meter along all edges, that cube or container would hold an amount of water which would weigh one gram. One gram was to be the basic unit of measurement of mass (weight).

Both the liter and the gram could be multiplied by tens and divided by tens in the same manner as the meter. In this way an entire system of measurement of distance, of volume, and of mass could be built from the meter.

Building such a key relationship between meter, liter, and gram, between length, volume, and mass, was a practical idea, and regardless of some errors, its simplicity and usefulness have made the metric system the most used system in the world.

Here is a table which shows what happens when we cube the seven most common metric measurements and how volume and mass (weight) are related to the meter:

Cubed Lengths	Liters	Grams
1 cubic meter	equals 1 kiloliter	equals 1,000 kilograms (of water)
100 cubic decimeters	equals 1 hectoliter	equals 100 kilograms (of water)
10 cubic decimeters	equals 1 dekaliter	equals 10 kilograms (of water)

Cubed Lengths	Liters	Grams
1 cubic decimeter	equals 1 liter	equals 1 kilogram (of water)
100 cubic centimeters	equals 1 deciliter	equals 100 grams (of water)
10 cubic centimeters	equals 1 centiliter	equals 10 grams (of water)
1 cubic centimeter	equals 1 milliliter	equals 1 gram (of water)

4.

The Liter

The liter is only two tablespoons larger than our customary quart. The liter is the most common amount of any liquid used everywhere in the world. Water, oil, beer, gasoline, wine, molasses, turpentine, soda, paint, and cough syrup are measured by the liter. Many liquids are bought, sold, and measured by the half or quarter liter. For the everyday measurement of common liquids this is all one needs to know.

When large amounts of a liquid must be measured, the kiloliter is sometimes used. In scientific work and even in the drugstore, the liter is too large an amount, and smaller measurements must be made. For these purposes the centiliter and the milliliter are popular. The centiliter is one-hundredth of a liter, and the milliliter is one-thousandth of a liter.

Here is a look at liquid measurement in table form:

1 kiloliter is 1,000 liters
1 liter is slightly larger than a quart
1 centiliter is 0.01 liter
1 milliliter is 0.001 liter

5.

The Gram

The gram and the kilogram are the only two words we must learn in order to handle everyday problems in the metric world of weight. A gram is about the weight of two small paper clips or a large lima bean. A thousand grams is called a kilogram. It might be convenient someday to order a half kilogram of hamburger or a kilogram and a quarter of sirloin steak.

In countries using the metric system many people have even dropped the word gram from kilogram. They often ask for a kilo of sugar or a half kilo of flour. This is, of course, a violation of metric style and standards. A kilo, as you know, is merely a thousand. However, there is a saying, ''Usage is king,'' and perhaps we will have to accept this and other deviations too.

A gram, though small, is too large an amount of matter for scientists to work with in many experiments. At the drugstore we can see clear evidence of this fact. There we find many bottles and boxes with the word milligram on them. Since milli- means thousand, milligram means a thousandth of a gram.

Here is the story in table form:

1 kilogram is 1,000 grams
1 gram is about the weight of two small paper clips
1 milligram is 0.001 gram

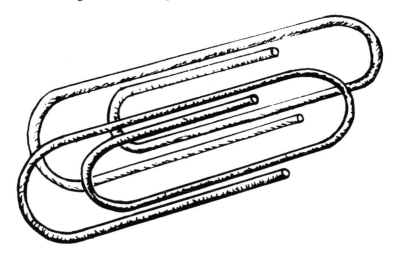

Two small paper clips will weigh just about 1 gram.

6.

In Sports

Long ago a great American track star won an Olympic broad-jumping event and lamented, "I've won, but I don't know how far I've jumped." The length of his leap had been announced in centimeters. Today athletes and spectators alike have mastered much of the metric lingo. Because most international sports events are measured and recorded in metric units, we have been forced to learn them. Centimeters, meters, and kilometers can be found regularly on most sports pages of most newspapers. Television and radio coverage of Olympic and other international contests has greatly increased.

Perhaps it is from the sports pages that many of us first learned about the metric system. Here, for example, are some items from a recent sports section of the New York *Times*:

Miss Young Wins
At 500 Meters
In Title Skating

29

Barron Wins 3000-Meter in 4:45.9
Heinz of Princeton Wins
One- and Three-Meter Dives

Of course these headlines merely require one to remember that a meter is slightly longer than a yard. Remembering, too, that 1,000 meters is a kilometer, it's easier to think of the 500-meter event as being a half kilometer, and the 3,000-meter event as being 3 kilometers. However, for a fuller comparison of metric distances commonly raced, here is a table of metric distances and their English equivalents:

50 meters	. . . .	164.04 feet
60 meters	. . . .	196.86 feet
100 meters	. . . .	328.1 feet
200 meters	. . . .	656.2 feet
300 meters	. . . .	984.3 feet
400 meters	. . . .	1,312.4 feet
500 meters	. . . .	1,640.5 feet
600 meters	. . . .	1,968.6 feet
800 meters	. . . .	2,624.7 feet
1,000 meters	. . . .	3,280.9 feet
1,500 meters	. . . .	4,921.3 feet
2,000 meters	. . . .	6,561.7 feet
3,000 meters	. . . .	9,842.6 feet
4,000 meters	. . . .	13,123.4 feet
5,000 meters	. . . .	16,404.3 feet
6,000 meters	. . . .	19,685.1 feet
7,000 meters	. . . .	22,966.0 feet
8,000 meters	. . . .	26,246.8 feet
9,000 meters	. . . .	29,527.0 feet
10,000 meters	. . . .	32,808.5 feet

If you are a coach or a runner and you wish to measure off a metric distance to practice for a meet, you may find this table useful. Steel tapes with metric units can also be purchased at larger sports-supply houses.

Next to the word meter, the most-often-used word expressing distance is the word kilometer. It is used in automobile and horse racing as well as in distance skiing, skating, track, and marathon events. How does it compare to a mile? Many people like to think of the kilometer as being a bit more than 6/10 of a mile. This is true, but the exact figure is 0.621372 of a mile. The kilometer is exactly 3,280.8 feet. Compare this to 5,280, which is the number of feet in a mile.

This type of item also may be found on sports pages:

John McCormack Drives
5-Liter Elfin Repko
To Win at Line Rick

You may have deciphered that the Elfin Repko is a sports car. But to what does 5 liters refer? First remember that a liter is slightly larger than a quart or, to be exact:

1 liter equals 1.0567 American liquid quarts
1 liquid quart equals 0.9463 liter

A five-liter car, then, is a car that has an engine in which the total volume swept out by the pistons is 5 liters. Put another way, it is the total volume of the cylinders measured between the top and bottom of their strokes. In the United States we have traditionally referred to this volume as so many cubic inches of piston displacement. The old B-24 airplane engine, which was called an R 1830, had radial engines, each of which had a piston displacement of 1,830 cubic inches. The phrase 5 liter is simply another way of expressing piston displacement or of giving you the capacity of an engine.

During an Olympic year or a year of pre-Olympic preparation you will find many metric words or units being bandied about. You may be interested to know that the shot used in the woman's shot put event must weigh exactly 4 kilograms (8 pounds 13 ounces). The men's shot must weigh 7.25 kilograms (16 pounds). The discus for men must weigh 2 kilograms, and for women 1 kilogram. The javelin must weigh 800 grams for men and 600 grams for women.

You may find it useful to think of a gram as being about the weight of two small paper clips or a large shelled peanut. More accurately, of course, you can remember that a gram is the weight of that amount of water that can be held in a container that equals a cubed centimeter. Of course you will have no difficulty now in remembering that a kilogram is 1,000 grams and that 4 kilograms is 4,000 grams.

Now let us suppose that you have just completed a broad jump of 5 meters 8 centimeters. You have only to remember that the centimeter is 1/100 of a meter. Or that you have high jumped and that the bar will be raised 1 decimeter. This might happen only in the early stages of a jumping competition. One decimeter is of course 1/10 of a meter. In high jumping or in any other event where progress is measured in centimeters it may be helpful to remember that 2-1/2 centimeters, or 2-1/2cm, is only slightly less than 1 inch.

Here is the exact relationship:

1 centimeter equals 0.39370 inches or roughly 4/10 of an
inch
1 inch equal 2.540 centimeters or roughly 2-1/2 centimeters

A common racing distance is the mile. Both men and
horses run the mile in the United States. How does it compare
with the kilometer? We saw before that the kilometer equals
3,280.8 feet or a bit more than 6/10 (0.621372) of a mile.
Reversing this, you can see that the mile is equal to 1-6/10
(1.60935) of a kilometer.
Or simply

1 kilometer equals 6/10 of a mile (roughly)
1 mile equals 1-6/10 of a kilometer (roughly)

Finally, what about football? Imagine a sports announcer
saying, "The Green Bay Packers have the ball. It's second
down and 8.21 meters to go." Of course it will be totally
unnecessary to change the football field or any part of the
game. Even if football were to become a great international
game, it would not be necessary to change it. For all time
it will be "First down and ten to go."
Soccer is reported to be the most popular sport inter-
nationally. Going metric with soccer presents no problem
because there is no standard size for a soccer field.
Nor will it be necessary to make any changes in baseball
or basketball. The basic dimensions of the court and the
diamond will not change and can be described in either
metric or customary units.

7.

At the Drugstore

Most of the items sold in drugstores today are measured in metric amounts. Some metric units, appearing on bottles, boxes, and tubes, we accept perhaps without understanding. For example, we buy 8mm, 16mm, or 35mm film. Few of us see the millimeter as 0.001 of a meter or as 0.1 centimeter.

Vitamins are a part of our diets. We may order a bottle of 50mg vitamin C, use them every day, and find it unnecessary to understand that mg means milligram.

Of course the drug companies that produce medicines and the doctors who prescribe them have long used metric measurements and their abbreviations. So have the research scientists and laboratory workers who help develop new drugs. The SI system is used by scientists in every country of the world. It enables them to communicate with one another and understand the experiments, as well as the results each secures. Everyone benefits from mutual use of the metric system.

Among research scientists, doctors, laboratory technicians, and druggists, the milligram is the most widely used measurement. However, it is far from the smallest unit in use. In addition to the milligram, which is the smallest unit of mass (weight) that we have discussed, you will find on some labels the abbreviation mc. These two letters appearing together refer to a still smaller unit of measurement. They stand for micro- which means 0.000001 part. It may refer to a microgram, a microliter, or a micrometer. In drug measurement it will refer to a microgram, a unit of mass (weight).

This tiny amount may appear on a label to represent, for example, the amount of Vitamin B^{12}. The label may read Vitamin B^{12}, 2mcg.

If a label or a prescription indicates a dosage of 5cc, the cc refers to cubic centimeter. A cubic centimeter, remember, is the volume that equals a milliliter. Five milliliters is equal to a teaspoon of liquid. In short, 5cc is the same as 5ml, which is roughly equal to a teaspoon. If you multiply this by 3 (5ml times 3), you of course have one tablespoon. Here is a table that may help in figuring the metric contents of some common household measures:

> 1 teaspoon is 5ml
> 1 dessert spoon is 8ml
> 1 tablespoon is 15ml
> 1 wineglass is 60ml
> 1 glass is 250 ml (8 ounces)

You may find the word minim on many labels too. This is not a metric unit. It is an old apothecary's term that comes from Latin and means least. It represented the least amount of a liquid that an apothecary (druggist) could handle. It was a rough representation of a drop. The minim today is not a drop. It is always 1/60 of a fluid dram or 1/20ml.

The drop, of course, is not usually prescribed as a dose in medicine. The drop varies greatly in size. Its size depends on the nature of the liquid being dropped, its viscosity, its temperature, and its specific gravity. When a doctor does prescribe drops, he also prescribes a special dropper for the medicine you are taking.

Some of the other abbreviations you will find on a prescription or a label are not metric at all but measurements of dosage intervals.

Here is a table that shows the abbreviations many doctors use to indicate time intervals for dosage:

> b.i.d. means two times per day
> t.i.d. means three times per day
> q.i.d. means four times per day
> ut. dict. means as directed
> a.c. means before meals
> p.c. means after meals
> o.d. means daily
> p.r.n. means when needed

The table presented below or a similar one, is used by your druggist when he makes up your prescription. It presents the approximate English apothecary units and their metric equivalents. Note that the English liquid units are (in descending order):

quarts
pints
ounces
drams
minims

Note too that the metric liquid units are all in milliliters (ml). Again, the English units of weight and mass are (in descending order): ounces, drams, and grains.

The metric units are all in grams (gm) and milligrams (mg).

Equivalents of Weights and Measures

LIQUID MEASURE

METRIC	APPROXIMATE APOTHECARY EQUIVALENTS	METRIC	APPROXIMATE APOTHECARY EQUIVALENTS
1000 ml	1 quart	3 ml	45 minims
750 ml	1½ pints	2 ml	30 minims
500 ml	1 pint	1 ml	15 minims
250 ml	8 fluid ounces	0.75 ml	12 minims
200 ml	7 fluid ounces	0.6 ml	10 minims
100 ml	3½ fluid ounces	0.5 ml	8 minims
50 ml	1¾ fluid ounces	0.3 ml	5 minims
30 ml	1 fluid ounce	0.25 ml	4 minims
15 ml	4 fluid drams	0.2 ml	3 minims
10 ml	2½ fluid drams	0.1 ml	1½ minims
8 ml	2 fluid drams	0.06 ml	1 minim
5 ml	1¼ fluid drams	0.05 ml	¾ minim
4 ml	1 fluid dram	0.03 ml	½ minim

37

WEIGHT

METRIC		APPROXIMATE APOTHECARY EQUIVALENTS		METRIC		APPROXIMATE APOTHECARY EQUIVALENTS	
30	Gm	.. 1	ounce	40	mg	... 2/3	grain
15	Gm	.. 4	drams	30	mg	... 1/2	grain
10	Gm	.. 2½	drams	25	mg	... 3/8	grain
7.5	Gm	.. 2	drams	20	mg	... 1/3	grain
6	Gm	.. 90	grains	15	mg	... 1/4	grain
5	Gm	.. 75	grains	12	mg	... 1/5	grain
4	Gm	.. 60	grains	10	mg	... 1/6	grain
			(1 dram)	8	mg	... 1/8	grain
3	Gm	.. 45	grains	6	mg	... 1/10	grain
2	Gm	.. 30	grains	5	mg	... 1/12	grain
			(1/2 dram)	4	mg	... 1/15	grain
1.5	Gm	.. 22	grains	3	mg	... 1/20	grain
1	Gm	.. 15	grains	2	mg	... 1/30	grain
0.75	Gm	.. 12	grains	1.5	mg	... 1/40	grain
0.6	Gm	.. 10	grains	1.2	mg	... 1/50	grain
0.5	Gm	.. 7½	grains	1	mg	... 1/60	grain
0.4	Gm	.. 6	grains	0.8	mg	... 1/80	grain
0.3	Gm	.. 5	grains	0.6	mg	... 1/100	grain
0.25	Gm	.. 4	grains	0.5	mg	... 1/120	grain
0.2	Gm	.. 3	grains	0.4	mg	... 1/150	grain
0.15	Gm	.. 2½	grains	0.3	mg	... 1/200	grain
0.12	Gm	.. 2	grains	0.25	mg	... 1/250	grain
0.1	Gm	.. 1½	grains	0.2	mg	... 1/300	grain
75	mg	... 1¼	grains	0.15	mg	... 1/400	grain
60	mg	... 1	grain	0.12	mg	... 1/500	grain
50	mg	... ¾	grain	0.1	mg	... 1/600	grain

8.

In the Home

Cooks in metric countries use the same kind of household utensils to measure ingredients as do cooks in the dwindling nonmetric world. Of course a pinch of anything is not the same everywhere. Neither are teaspoons, tablespoons, or cups, which come in bewildering sizes and shapes. Only cups and spoons made for measuring will give us accurate amounts. Perhaps even these should be checked.

While it is reasonable to assume that these common utensils will continue to be used for a long time, it is equally reasonable to assume that the pressure to learn their metric values will grow. The pressure to use metric units will come to the kitchen slowly but just as surely as elsewhere. It will be a beneficial change. The confusion between liquid ounces and avoirdupois ounces will die a natural but lingering death. So will the pint that weighs a pound and the peck; also the gill and the dram. What we will have eventually is the simple gram and the liter.

Where will this pressure develop? No doubt some of it will come from food processors, packagers, and suppliers. They may find it increasingly profitable to package and label their products in metric units. Also, in time those who have been reared with and taught the SI system in school may very well come to insist on SI measurements in the kitchen as well as in the rest of the home.

In the meantime we who may have to cook in the time of transition may need considerable help. We must try to keep the old English units straight and learn the metric ones too. Fortunately the metric ones are easy enough to learn. It is the necessity to learn conversions or the relationships between the two that can cause a bit of trouble. Here is a small table that may be of some help:

Volume or Liquid Equivalents

SI		OLD STYLE
Milliliter (ml)	Ounces	Common Containers
5 milliliters	1/6	1 teaspoon (tsp)
15 milliliters	1/2	1 tablespoon (tbs)
30 milliliters	1	2 tbs
240 milliliters	8	1 cup
1/4 liter (approx.)	8-1/2	1 cup plus 1 tbs
480 milliliters	16	1 pint
960 milliliters	32	1 quart
1 liter	33	1 quart plus 2 tbs

Recall that a milliliter is a 1/1,000 of a liter. A milli- of anything, be it meter, liter, or gram, is a thousandth part. Recall, too, that 10 milliliters equals 1 centiliter (which is 1/100 of a liter).

You will notice that while in the metric column above

most items appear in milliliters, they could easily be changed. Fifteen milliliters could obviously be 1-1/2 centiliters. Thirty milliliters could be 3 centiliters. Nine hundred and sixty milliliters could be expressed as 9 deciliters 6 centiliters or simply 9d 6c. None of these changes is necessary, however. The list in milliliters adequately conveys a picture of increasing volume.

Another interesting thing about the above milliliter column is that since one milliliter of water weighs (for all practical purposes) one gram, each of the items could be changed to milligrams. It may be of only occasional value in cooking to realize that one milliliter of water equals or has a mass (weight) of one gram. Of course we must not forget that this is true only of water. Five milliliters or one teaspoon of molasses or of mercury will definitely be of greater mass (weight) than water.

In that connection here are a few mass (weight) equivalents that just might help solve some culinary crisis—or make understandable some label in the medicine cabinet.

SI		OLD STYLE
1 milligram	equals	0.0154 grain
1 gram	equals	0.0353 ounce
1 kilogram	equals	2.205 pounds

Here are a couple of recipes that you might like to try.* They may help you to start cooking in the metric manner.

*From "Think Metric", an article in the January, 1973, issue of *House Beautiful*. Copyright © 1973 The Hearst Corporation.

If you would like to equip your kitchen with metric measuring spoons, cups, glasses, bottles, and scales, they are available now at some large household-supply houses and even some department stores. If your own local store doesn't carry them, perhaps it will order them for you.

Here is a recipe from Italy:

Saltimbocca all' Emiliana
(Veal Scaloppine from Emilia)

1 kilogram fresh spinach	Freshly ground pepper
(four 250-gram bags)	1 level teaspoon sage
3 eggs	1/2 tablespoon (about 5
1/8 liter olive oil	sprigs) chopped parsley
1 kilogram veal scaloppine	100 grams butter
(12 slices)	12 thin, lean slices prosciutto
Flour	4 tablespoons Marsala wine
Salt	

Wash the spinach and strip off any heavy stems. Drop into a large kettle (not aluminum) of boiling salted water. Boil hard, uncovered, for exactly three minutes. Drain and set aside. Hard-cook the eggs, and then cool, peel and cut them into wedges. Set them aside, too.

Heat the olive oil in a large skillet. Dip each scaloppine in flour, shaking off any excess. Sauté quickly, a few at a time, until golden brown on both sides. As they are cooked, lay them flat in a roasting pan. Sprinkle with salt and pepper, the sage and parsley and dot with 80 grams of the butter. Place a piece of prosciutto on top of each scaloppine. Keep warm in a low oven.

Discard the oil from the skillet. Add the remaining butter and sauté the spinach until piping hot through. Do not overcook. Make a bed of the hot spinach on a large heated serving platter. Finally, pour the 4 tablespoons Marsala into the skillet and reduce slightly.

To serve, arrange the slices of scaloppine and prosciutto on top of the hot spinach. Garnish with the hard-cooked eggs, and pour the Marsala sauce over all. Serves six.

This recipe is from Brazil:

Bifa con Molho
(Beef with Sauce)

900 grams to 1 kilogram fillet of beef
Salt
Freshly ground pepper
100 grams (3/4 stick) butter
4 medium yellow onions, peeled and sliced thin
1/8 liter beef broth, heated

Have the butcher slice the meat into 12 slices; then flatten them slightly. Salt and pepper the steaks.

Heat about half the butter in a large heavy skillet. Brown the steaks, a few at a time, very quickly on both sides. As they brown, lift to a heated serving platter; keep warm. Add butter as needed.

Add the remaining butter to the skillet; then add the onions. Fry over medium heat, stirring well to loosen all the brown encrustations in the bottom of the pan. When onions are brown and tender, add the hot broth. Bring to a boil. Then simmer for five minutes. Season with salt and pepper to taste, and pour the sauce over the steaks. Serve immediately. Serves about six.

American winemakers may have already begun the switchover to bottles of metric sizes. Pints, quarts, gallons, and even the fifth may have begun a slow march to oblivion. Recently the powerful California Winegrowers Institute proposed that U.S. winemakers at least consider the switch to metric bottles. The heads of that institute have suggested the following bottle sizes:

> quarter liter
> half liter
> three-quarter liter
> liter
> two liters
> three liters
> four liters

If you will consult the table of Volume or Liquid Equivalents presented earlier in this chapter, you will see that one liter quals one quart plus two tablespoons. You will also find there the one-quarter liter and other equivalents, which should help you understand these suggested metric bottle sizes.

In dress patterns, some companies began using the SI system of measurements along with the old style a few years ago.

Here are some suggested sizes for various items of clothing that are under consideration to be made in world standard sizes. Of course there are dozens of systems of measurement of these items in use around the world. While these metric sizes have not yet become official standards, you may find it interesting to compare them to present United States sizes.

SHOES

Women			Men	
Metric	*U.S.*		*Metric*	*U.S.*
34	4		38	6
35	5		40	7
36	6		41	8
38	7		43	9
38.5	8		44	10
40	9		45	11
41	10		46	12

HATS

53	21		52	6½
56	22		54	6¾
58	23		56	7
61	24		58	7¼
62	24½		60	7½

STOCKINGS—SOCKS

0	8		23	9
2	9		25.5	10
4	10		28	11
6	11		29.25	11½
			30.5	12

DRESSES		SHIRTS	
38	10	33	13
40	12	35	14
42	14	37	15
44	16	40	16
46	18	42	17
48	20		

9.

In Your Craft, Hobby, or Workshop

Whether you have an elaborate workshop equipped with machinery or a simple table and a few tools, you may find it rewarding to switch to SI there. In fact, it may be the best place to go metric first, for doing has always been one of the most reliable ways of learning.

You'll need a couple of new tools. A full meterstick or steel rule that is calibrated in millimeters will serve well when making longer measurements. The other basic tool should be a short rule 10 or 20 centimeters long. In order to avoid distracting you, neither of these rules should have the old inch calibrations on one edge. In some places it may be difficult to secure such rules. In that event cover the old inch calibration with a piece of tape. If you are working with leather or cloth, you may want to secure a metric cloth tape. These are easy to secure and quite inexpensive.

Don't be surprised either, after a short period of use, if you discover that these basic tools are easier to use than the old inch-foot rules. You will not have to cope with the addition, subtraction, and multiplication of such fractions as 3/32 or 5/64. Thinking in terms of tens and decimals can quickly become a habit. It will only be necessary to remember that meters are divided by tens to get decimeters, centimeters, and millimeters. In table form:

1 meter divides into 10 decimeters
1 decimeter divides into 10 centimeters
1 centimeter divides into 10 millimeters

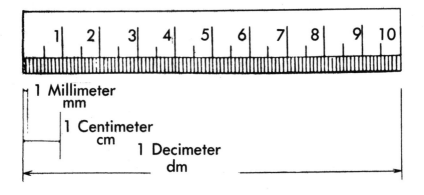

A 10 centimeter (or 1 decimeter) rule.

Here is a ten-centimeter rule, or one decimeter, whichever we wish to name it. You can see that if you had ten of these rulers laid end to end, they would equal in length one meter.

Not all projects can be made with a few hand tools, of course. Eventually you may want to make more complicated things, some of which will require machinery. For example, you may be using a plan that calls for three holes one centimeter deep. Since the drill press has a scale at the depth gauge that is calibrated in inches and fractions, this will present a small problem. Not a large one.

The solution might be, if very great accuracy is not required, simply to remember that one centimeter is but a hair more than 3/8 inch and proceed to drill. A better solution might be to cover the old scale or add a temporary metric one alongside. White tape, paper, or cardboard can be marked with metric units and pasted in place. Printed and pressure-sensitive metric tape is also purchasable. Still another possible solution is to make a new scale of aluminum or brass and fasten it to the machine with the same screws that held the old ones in place. Wherever this will work, the metal can be marked with a chisel and the chisel marks darkened with ink. Pehaps other of your shop machines can be altered in the same manner. Of course, many companies produce both English and metric scales for their machines and will be glad to sell metric scales to you.

At this point, too, it may already have occurred to you that sooner or later we're going to need metric twist drills. While they are not now available in most hardware stores, you can order them from some large supply houses. In the meantime, especially if you have full (or partial) sets of letter, number, and alphabet sizes, you can consolidate the appropriate ones into a metric set. Use an outside caliper and a metric rule to select those individual drills that will be most useful.* A color code can also be devised to help identify the most-often-used sizes. Along with the converted depth-gauge scale on the drill press, this will enable you to drill metric-size holes to metric depths.

As you may already know, most of the companies that manufacture lathes, millers, surface grinders, and other machines also manufacture metric machines and the equipment to convert English-style machines to metric. Some of this is done for foreign markets. The lathe, for example, can be changed or converted to cut metric threads by installing two gears with the correct number of teeth in the power train (between the stud and lead screw gears). These are called transposing gears and, along with the metric cellar scales for the compound rest and cross-reed, can be purchased and installed without much difficulty. Most lathe manuals contain fairly detailed instructions for cutting metric threads and for changing gears.

Similar solutions can be found to the problems of converting scales on millers, shapers, grinders, and other machines. First consult the manufacturer to see how much help he can give you, and then do some improvising on your own.

Here are some tapping and clearance sizes for ISO metric coarse thread series:

For general purposes the tapping drill size is obtained by subtracting the pitch from the nominal major diameter. Thus for the 12mm diameter the pitch is 1.75mm and the tapping drill size is 1025mm. All dimensions here are in millimeters.

*See conversion table in the back of this book.

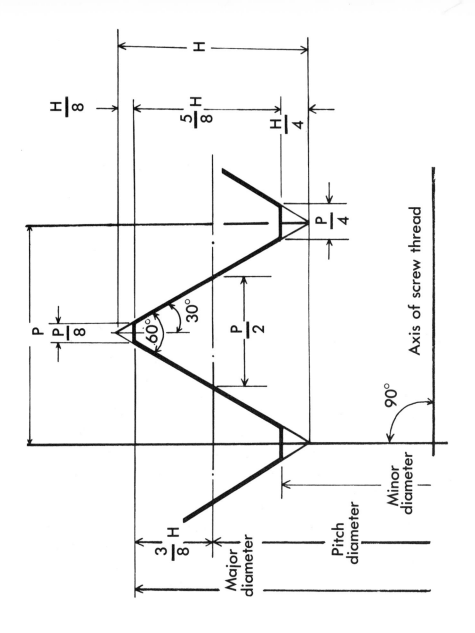

The basic form of ISO metric thread.

Key to symbols: p = pitch. H = 0.866 03p (depth of fundamental triangle). H/8 = 0.108 25p. H/4 = 0.216 51p. 3/8H = 0.324 76p. 5/8 H = 0.541 27p.

Diameter	Pitch	Tapping Drill	Clearance Drill
2	0·4	1·6	2·2
2·5	0·45	2·05	2·6
3	0·5	2·5	3·2
4	0·7	3·3	4·2
5	0·8	4·2	5·2
6	1·0	5·0	6·2
8	1·25	6·75	8·2
10	1·5	8·5	10·2
(11)	1·5	9·5	11·2
12	1·75	10·25	12·2

If you are going metric in the arts and crafts field, where you may be using plaster, water, and enameling powders, or in ceramics, where you are using clay, water, and glazes, or in art, where you may be mixing various and sundry items, you'll want to practice with liters and grams instead of ounces and pounds. This will not be a difficult step.

First you'll need a beam scale for determining mass (weight) in grams. This can sometimes be borred. If you don't have one, you'll find it is easy to make. Man has been making simple beam scales out of various materials for thousands of years. Find a stick about 50 centimeters long (or longer) and balance it on a sharp-edged object that will serve as a fulcrum. Make a mark at the center of the stick or the balancing point. Place other marks exactly the same distance from each end of the stick where you will suspend pans. These pans can be made from identical can lids. Suspend them from the beam with either string or wire. Next cut some pieces of lead, solder, or clay, and weigh them on a spring scale. Cut a few that will weigh one gram each, then one a hectogram, and one a kilogram.

Here is a conversion table that will help you:

1 gram equals 0.035 ounce (approx. advp.)
1 ounce equals 28 grams
1 hectogram equals .35 ounce
1 kilogram equals 35. or 2.2 pounds (approx.)

If and when your plans call for liters and deciliters, you can make your own measuring containers too. Of course metric containers can be bought at drug, medical, and scientific supply houses or borrowed from someone. Making your own, however, can be rewarding in terms of pleasure as well as education.

First, measure out a liter of water (see the chapter "In the Home" for conversion table) and pour it into a large enough can or glass container. Mark the level of the water surface on the side of the container in ink. Next, divide the distance between the mark and the bottom of the container into ten equal-sized spaces. Each of these spaces will represent a deciliter. For smaller divisions you will need small containers.

If you are an artist, draftsman, or printer, you will be using paper of various sizes. The international committee that meets periodically to adopt standards for the metric world has suggested that to secure a reduction in the number of paper sizes and to achieve some international order, paper

manufacturers, for general use, should produce eight standard sizes. Here are those sizes pictured. Perhaps only
three or four of these will ever be in common use. If you
wish, you can cut paper to these metric sizes or to the
nearest metric size that is convenient for you to use.

PAPER

Recommended Sizes for General Use

Designation	mm	inches
A0	841 x 1189	33 x 47
A1	594 x 841	23½ x 33
A2	420 x 594	16½ x 23½
A3	297 x 420	11¼ x 16½
A4	210 x 297	8¼ x 11¾
A5	148 x 210	5¾ x 8¼
A6	105 x 148	4⅛ x 5¾
A7	74 x 105	2⅞ x 4⅛

In addition to using metric-size paper, you may, if you
wish, in your math work, mechanical drawing, and shop
work generally, use graph or grid paper that is lined to
form the following metric squares:

5mm or 10mm squares for orthographic work
5mm or 10mm squares for diagonal ruling for oblique
  views
5mm or 10mm squares for isometric work
5mm or 10mm squares for axonometric drawings

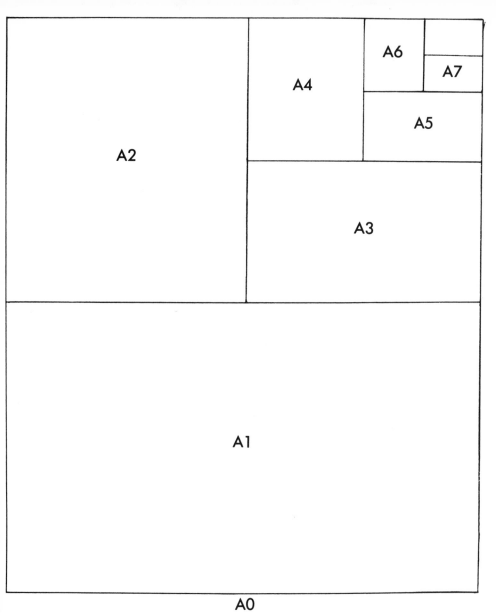

Recommended paper sizes (ISO) for general use.

If you wish to go another step in the metric direction, you can make drawings to scales that are decimal and not fractional or duodecimal. You can use 2:1, 5:1, 10:1, and 15:1 or 1:2 or 1:5, etc.

10.

In Science

The metric system has been used by scientists in all parts of the world for many years. It has become a kind of common language shared by scientists and has made the exchange of information much easier. No doubt mankind has benefited. However, along with new methods of conquering disease and prolonging life, the scientific world has also been better able to share such horrors as new atomic weapons, chemical techniques for destroying crops, and new kinds of guns.

Regardless of some of the uses to which the metric system has been put, many scientists feel that in a small way at least it offers the possibility of greater understanding among peoples. A shared discovery that prevents the spread of a dreaded disease no doubt creates a shared feeling of good-will. At a very minimum level our shared use of the meter, liter, and gram will enable our young scientists to learn to measure easier and faster.

Of the three ways of measuring, with meter, liter, and gram, it is only the gram that a scientist uses differently from the nonscientist or the layman. The scientist uses the gram to measure mass. We who are nonscientists most often use the word weight instead of mass. Even in the daily newspaper and in many magazine articles we now find the word mass. It is extremely useful to understand the difference between weight and mass.

Perhaps it is at the supermarket or the fruit and vegetable stand that we most often see both mass and weight measured. There we often find two kinds of scales.

One kind is a simple spring scale. On it is a single pan hung from a spring. When, for example, we place bananas on the pan, the spring is stretched and moves a hand on a dial. The hand tells us how much the bananas weigh. The word weigh is correct here because a spring scale measures the pull of gravity on an object. Since gravitational pull is less as we go outward from the center of the earth, an object will weigh less as it is moved outward from the earth's center. Thus a buch of bananas will weigh slightly less on a mountaintop than at sea level. The amount of bananas will not change, but their weight will. Scientists need a more reliable method of measuring the amount of bananas—or anything else.

This is why scientists use a beam scale for measuring the amount of matter in an object. This kind of scale can also be found at the supermarket. A beam scale consists, in its elementary form, of a long arm or beam that has a known amount of matter or mass at one end and the unknown mass at the other end. This is a two-pan scale that is balanced or supported only at the center of the beam. When the unknown object equals the known object in mass, the beam is level and the unknown mass becomes known.

Gravity is not a factor here because it pulls equally at both ends of the beam. The only difference between the two masses is the amount of matter in them. The word mass refers to the amount of matter in an object. The word weight refers to the pull of gravity on an object, a pull that will vary according to the object's location.

Another thing that separates scientists from laymen is that the scientist must measure many extremely small amounts and also many extremely large or distant items. In scientific experiments many things must be investigated that are smaller than a millimeter, a milliliter, or a milligram. Tiny forms of life such as bacteria and the cells of plants must be measured. Inadequate, too, are the kilometer, kiloliter, and kilogram. The vast distances from our earth to the stars in the galaxies must also be measured. Both the kilo- and the milli- are inadequate for these extremes. To handle them the metric system has had to be expanded.

Use All Prefixes with All Units
(Meters, Grams, or Liters)

Multiplication Factors	Prefix	Symbol
$1\ 000\ 000\ 000\ 000 = 10^{12}$	tera	T
$1\ 000\ 000\ 000 = 10^{9}$	giga	G
$1\ 000\ 000 = 10^{6}$	mega	M
$1\ 000 = 10^{3}$	kilo	k
$100 = 10^{2}$	hecto	h
$10 = 10^{1}$	deca	da
1	gram (or meter or liter)	

0.1 =	10^{-1}	deci	d
0.01 =	10^{-2}	centi	c
0.001 =	10^{-3}	milli	m
0.000 001 =	10^{-6}	micro	μ
0.000 000 001 =	10^{-9}	nano	n
0.000 000 000 001 =	10^{-12}	pico	p
0.000 000 000 000 001 =	10^{-15}	femto	f
0.000 000 000 000 000 001 =	10^{-18}	atto	a

As can be seen from this table, the system has been expanded in units of one thousand. The mega- (either meter, liter, or gram) represents an amount that is one thousand times the kilo-. The giga- is one thousand times the mega-, and the tera- is one thousand times the giga-.

Over the years, in some branches of science, even these expanded parts of the metric system have not proved equal to the total needs of the scientific world. In astronomy, for example, where almost unbelievable distances are now being measured, scientists rely on such units as the light-year. A light-year is, of course, the distance that light travels in one year. Since light travels at a rate of 186,272 miles per second, this is a very large unit of measurement. Scientists also use the parsec, a unit that represents 3.26 light-years.

Still another area of measurement that separates the layman from the scientist, particularly in the United States, is the area of temperature measurement. We ordinary mortals have grown accustomed to the face of the Fahrenheit thermometer. We know that freezing is 32° and that boiling, when we can remember it, is 212°. But most of the people in the world do not use the Fahrenheit thermometer either for everyday use or for scientific work. They use the Celsius thermometer. This is an easier tool to understand and to use.

On the Celsius thermometer 0 represents the freezing point of water and 100 represents the boiling point. Sometimes, and incorrectly now, this thermometer is called the centigrade thermometer. The word centigrade you may recognize as coming from the Latin and meaning 100 steps. This refers to the fact that water on this thermometer is a liquid from 0 to 100°. Below that it is a solid (ice), and above that it is a gas (steam). This is a very convenient measuring tool for scientists who must often work not only with water but also with many tissues and solids in which water is present. You will find it convenient too.

The man who invented this thermometer was Anders Celsius. He was a Swedish astronomer who first used the centigrade scale in 1742. By worldwide agreement it is now called the Celsius thermometer, and it is used by most people to satisfy their everyday needs as well as by scientists everywhere.

Still another temperature-measuring system has now been adopted by scientists of the metric countries. They must, of course, measure many extremes of temperature. For their purposes they have adopted the Kelvin or thermodynamic scale.

Other new standards have also been adopted by the SI committee that represents metric countries, not only for temperature but also for most other areas of measurement. This has been made both possible and necessary as a result of the tremendous improvement that has taken place in the

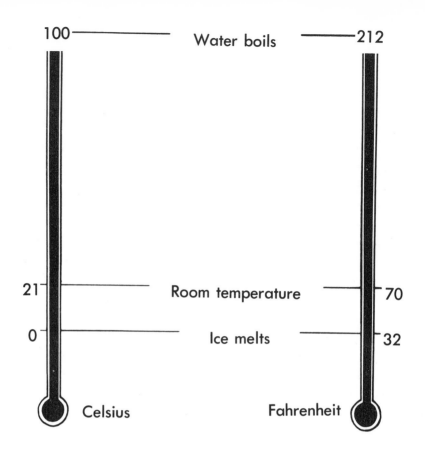

100 ——————— Water boils ——————212

21 —————— Room temperature —————— 70

0 —————— Ice melts —————— 32

Celsius   Fahrenheit

The metric (Celsius) thermometer compared to the Fahrenheit thermometer. In the more practical gradations of the Celsius, 0 equals freezing and 100 equals boiling point.

tools and ways of measuring. The eminent scientists who first adopted standards for the meter, the liter, and the gram made some errors. This is not unusual; the history of measurement has been a history of errors. Progress in any area has usually revealed the mistakes of the past. However, here are the present standards that enable people all over the world to have the same meter, gram, and liter, as well as many other units of measurement.

Meter (m): Length

The meter will be 1,650,763.73 wavelengths in vacuum of the orange-red line of the spectrum of krypton-86.

Kilogram (k): Mass

The standard for the unit of mass is a cylinder of platinum-iridium alloy kept by the International Bureau of Weights and Measures in Paris, France.

Liter (1): Volume

In 1964 at a General Conference on Weights and Measures the liter was redefined as exactly 1,000 cubic centimeters. Since it is derived from the centimeter, which is not a basic SI unit, the liter cannot be considered a basic SI unit. However, the liter is generally used almost everywhere as a metric unit of volume or capacity.

Kelvin (K): Temperature

The Kelvin or thermodynamic scale of temperature has its origin or zero point at absolute zero and has a fixed point defined as 273.16 kelvins.

Second (s): Time

One second will be the duration of 9,192,631,770 cycles of the radiation associated with a specified transition of the cesium atom.

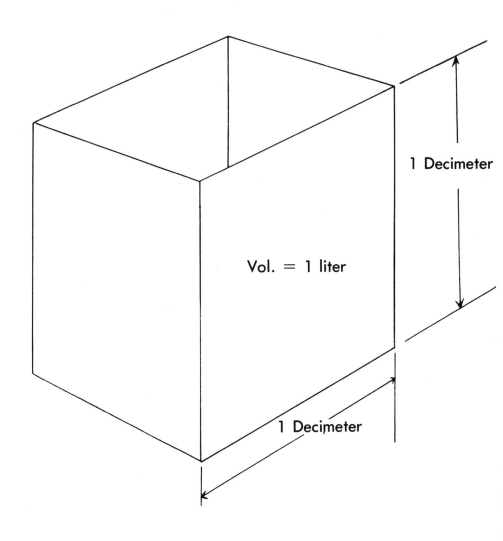

1 Decimeter

Vol. = 1 liter

1 Decimeter

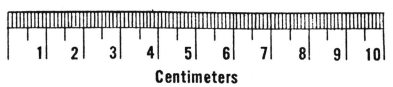

Centimeters

Ampere (A): Electric Current

The ampere is defined as the magnitude of the current that when flowing through each of two long parallel wires separated by one meter in free space results in a force between the wires of 2 x 10 $^{-7}$ newton for each meter of length.

Candela (cd): Luminous Intensity

The candela is defined as the luminous intensity of 1/600,000 of a square meter of a radiating cavity at the temperature of freezing platinum (2 042K).

Since some of the above definitions introduce terms with which not everyone is familiar, here is a very brief (perhaps too brief) explanation. First about the meter. The word krypton appears in this definition. This is the name of a gas that is number 36 on the list of elements that make up our universe. When this gas is heated, the colored light it radiates appears in waves. These waves are dependable and constant, and they can be measured. Scientists anywhere in the world can produce the orange-red light referred to, measure the wavelengths, and then multiply them by the number of times indicated. In this way scientists anywhere can reproduce the same meter.

The standard for the kilogram is a cylinder-shaped piece of metal that is kept in a special vault where it is protected from moisture and chemical damage and from temperature changes. People anywhere, remembering that a kilogram is 1,000 grams, and that one gram is the weight of water contained in a cubic centimeter, can make their own approximation of a kilogram. However, to know finally if they

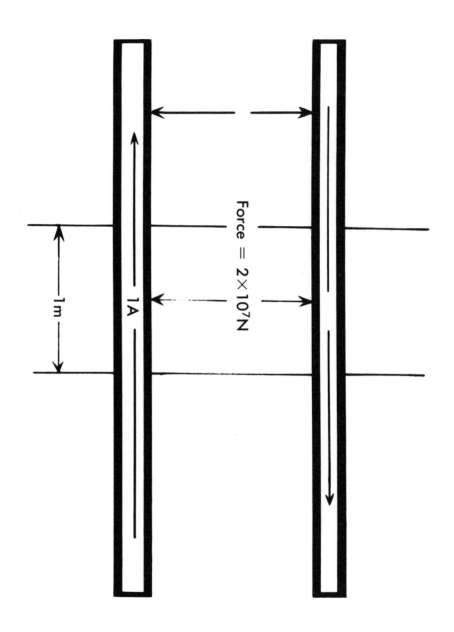

The Ampere (A), basic unit of electric current.

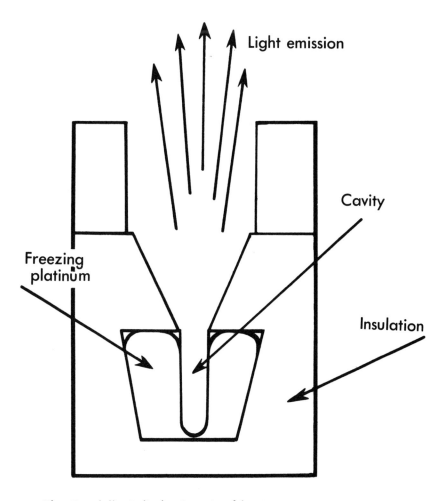

Light emission

Cavity

Freezing
platinum

Insulation

The Candella (cd), basic unit of luminous intensity.

have measured accurately, they must compare it with the platinum-iridium cylinder maintained in Paris.

While the kelvin is the official metric unit of measurement for temperature, the Celsius thermometer is widely used everywhere. There is no conflict between the two systems, and the Celsius is generally considered a part of the metric system. The kelvin was named after Lord William Kelvin, an English physicist, who died in 1907. He discovered, among other things, that when a piece of metal undergoes a temperature change or when two differing temperatures occur in a piece of metal, an electromagnetic force is created. On the Kelvin scale, zero marks what is called absolute zero, a temperature at which all molecular activity ceases. The Kelvin scale is used mainly by scientists who must make minute measurements at extremes of temperature.

Here is a comparison of Kelvin, Celsius, and Fahrenheit

	Kelvin	Celsius	Fahrenheit
Absolute zero	0	−273.15	−459.67
Water freezes	273.15	0	32
Body temperature	310.15	37	98.6
Water boils	373.15	100	212

The standard for one second of time contains the word cesium. This is an alkali metal and a basic element that was discovered by Robert Bunsen, also the inventor of the popular Bunsen burner. A German scientist, he made many important contributions. The word transition here refers to the changed or excited state of the cesium atom at which time it radiates energy in cycles that can be counted. When the indicated number of cycles of radiation have occurred, that unit of time is one second.

The ampere is a word with which most of us are familiar. Here it is a unit of electrical current that was named for André Ampère, the French physicist. The word newton is a unit of force named after the famous Isaac Newton, who has been erroneously reported to have drawn a number of important conclusions simply because an apple fell upon his head. Here, however, 1 newton equals 1 kilogram-meter per second squared. In short, when a certain current flows through the two wires, there is an electrical force created between the two wires. When this force reaches the figure stated, there is 1 ampere flowing through each of the two wires.

All these standards, except for the liter, are called basic standards. However, many other things must be measured. For example, area, volume, acceleration, velocity, density, torque, thermal conductivity, electric charge, magnetic flux, luminous flux, to name but a few. These are measured with what are called derived units. They are units that come from a combination of the basic standards explained above. For example, acceleration is measured by a derived unit called meters per second squared. This is possible because our basic standards include both a standard for a meter and for a second. Density is measured by a derived unit called the kilogram per cubic meter. Both the kilogram and the meter are basic units.

Scientists all over the world use these many agreed-upon derived units to carry on their special investigations. Both the basic and the derived units have become a common language in the scientific community. They have certainly simplified scientific work and hopefully make it possible to achieve greater understanding.

11.

Land and Surface Measurements

The metric system makes land and surface measurements quite simple. How many of us are certain of the size of an acre or remember the number of yards in a rod? Or how many rods make an acre? For many of us the old English acre will forever remain another English mystery.

Fortunately you have only to understand two words to understand most measurements of land in the metric manner. One is are. The are is a piece of land that measures 10 meters on each side. Of course since 10 times 10 is 100, an are contains 100 square meters of land. The other word, an equally simple one, is the hectare. The hectare is exactly 100 ares. So that is most of the story of land measurements. The are is 10 meters by 10 meters, and the hectare is 100 ares.

It is the hectare that is the most popular and most commonly used unit of land measurement in metric countries. Naturally you'll occasionally hear someone use a simple fraction and speak about 1½ or 2¼ hectares, but mostly the word hectare is used alone.

Of course that are can be divided into its 100 smaller parts, each one meter square, and these are called centares. So looked at in another way, 1 square meter is a centare, 100 centares is 1 are, and 100 ares is 1 hectare.

In table form:

100 centares equal 1 are
100 ares equal 1 hectare

12.

Maps, Charts, and Sign-posts

Everyone, at some time or another, needs a map, a chart, or a signpost. Maps help us find our way over land, charts on water or in air, and signposts wherever strange roads cross. Traveling is a popular and necessary part of life. Since most of the world is metric, so are most of the signposts, charts, and maps. Reading them correctly may be more than important; it may be a matter of life and death.

You will be able to figure distances on a map or chart easily if you know how to use the scale you find there. A scale helps us understand the difference between the size of the map and the size of the earth that is mapped. A mapmaker knows the size of the area he is mapping and the size of the map he is making. To find the scale, he simply divides the size of the area by the size of the map.

For example, if he is making a map 50 centimeters wide and the area is 1,400 meters wide, he merely divides 50 into 1,400 to secure the number 28. The scale will be 1cm to 28 meters. Here you can see that 1cm being 1/100 of a meter, you have only to multiply both the 1 and the 28 by 100 to find the relationship or scale in the same

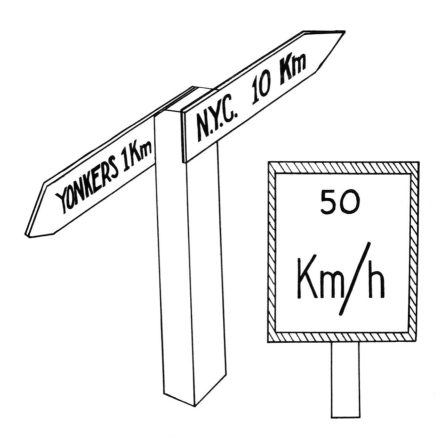

Road signs throughout the world are metric. Many signs on American highways now give miles and kilometers.

units. In this way the scale becomes 1m to 2,800m. Again, just divide the size of the area by the size of the map or chart.

Maps and charts also show a measured scale that gives you the length of the meter or the kilometer on the map. This meter or kilometer has been reduced to the size of a meter or kilometer on the map. Using the dividers or

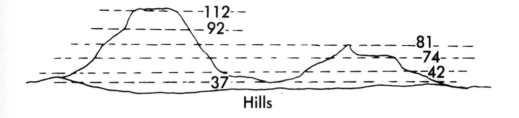

Hills

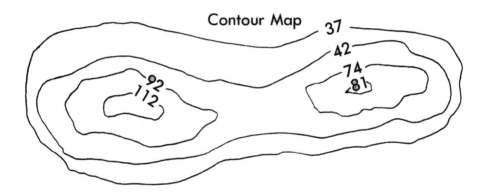

Contour Map

Contour maps record the number of meters above sea level for each change in ground elevation.

a compass divider or a rule made from the scale, you can figure out the distances on any part of the map.

Topographical maps are especially useful at times because they indicate the height and the specific nature of the land. Such maps often have the altitude above sea level marked in meters. Here is such a map.

Automobile and train trips in most countries of the world also require that we be familiar with the metric system. Not only maps and travel guides but also signposts will be marked in either meters or kilometers. Since you are now very familiar with the fact that a kilometer is 1,000 meters, it shouldn't surprise you to stumble over a sign marked 2½ kilometers. The ½ you would instantly recognize as being 500 meters.

Weather maps may contain metric measurements, too. There are continuous black lines on weather maps which are called isobars. They show the continuous area where the air pressure is the same (and different). Iso- comes from a Greek word meaning equal. Wherever you see this word you will know that it means "the same." Marked on the isobars are numbers that tell us the pressure of the air in millibars. The bar in millibar is a unit of pressure (1,000,000 dynes per square centimeter). A dyne is a unit of force. Specifically it is that force that, acting on a body of mass of one gram for one second, gives it a change in velocity of one centimeter per second. Now you can see that the bar, which is a unit of pressure, has been divided into a thousand smaller units, each called a millibar. Since most weather reports still give the air pressure in inches of mercury, here is a table that shows how they are related:

1 bar equals 29.6 inches of mercury
1 millibar equals 0.0296 inch of mercury

Finally, navigators, in order to find their way, still use

compasses, latitude and longitude lines, and the degrees of a circle, all of which are not metric. There have been and are some attempts to change the 360-degree circle to a 200- or a 400-degree circle so that the divisions could be decimal. So far these attempts have not been successful.

13.

Addition, Subtraction, and Multiplication

Because of the decimal nature of the metric system, you will be able to compute more easily with metric units than with our old English units. In the beginning, however, you will have to spend some time familiarizing yourself with the metric abbreviations. They are not difficult to learn. Here is a partial table of common abbreviations that will help you to begin computations.

Combine them in this manner:

gram: g	kilogram: kg
liter: 1	kiloliter: kl
meter: m	kilometer: km
kilo: k	and
hecto: h	decimeter: dm
deka: dk	centimeter: cm
deci: d	millimeter: mm
centi: c	etc.
milli: m	

The same methods are used in computing metric units as in English units. Here in brief is how we add metric units.

Vertical form:

3cm 6mm
4cm 6mm
7cm 12mm equals 8cm 2mm

Horizontal form:

(3cm 6mm) plus (4cm 6mm)
        equals (3cm 6mm) plus (4cm 6mm)
        equals (3cm plus 4cm) plus (6mm plus 6mm)
        equals 7cm plus 12mm
        equals (7cm plus 1cm) plus 2mm
        equals (8cm plus 2mm) or 8cm 2mm

Here is how scientists often take advantage of the decimal nature of the metric system. Using the same problem:

3.6mm
4.6mm
8.2mm or 8cm 2mm

You can do all this whenever all the measurements of a problem are expressed in the same units. Using the decimal point simply indicates that the number to the left is the next higher multiple of 10, which in this case is a centimeter (cm). Remember, deci-, centi-, milli-.

Here in brief is how we subtract metric units. The problem: Find the difference when we subtract 5cm 4mm from 8cm 5mm.

$$
\begin{array}{c}
8\text{cm}\,5\text{mm} \\
-5\text{cm}\,4\text{mm} \\
\hline
3\text{cm}\,1\text{mm}
\end{array}
\quad \text{or} \quad
\begin{array}{c}
8.5\text{mm} \\
5.4\text{mm} \\
\hline
3.1\text{mm}
\end{array}
$$

Another problem: What is the difference when we subtract 2m 6cm from 4m 3dm 8cm?

$$
\begin{array}{rcl}
4\text{m } 3\text{dm } 8\text{cm} &=& 4.38\text{m} \\
2\text{m } 0\text{dm } 6\text{cm} &=& 2.06 \\
\hline
& & 2.32\text{m}
\end{array}
$$

Here in brief is how metric units are multiplied:
Problem: Compute the product of 7 times 1m 3dm 4cm 5mm.

$$
\begin{array}{rcl}
1\text{m } 3\text{dm } 4\text{cm } 5\text{mm} &=& 1.345\text{m} \\
& & \underline{\times 7} \\
& & 9.415\text{m}
\end{array}
$$

Another problem: Compute the product of 4 times 2m 4dm.

$$
\begin{array}{rcl}
2\text{m } 4\text{dm} &=& 2.4\text{m} \\
& & \underline{\times 4} \\
& & 9.6\text{m}
\end{array}
$$

In this problem you can see that 4dm is also 4/10 of a

79

meter, so we have simply placed the decimal point between the 2 and the 4.

Here is how division is done in metric units:

Problem: Divide 4m 4dm 5cm 2mm by 2.

$$4.452m \div 2$$

$$\begin{array}{r} 2.226m \\ 2 \overline{)4.452m} \end{array}$$

As an earlier table in this book showed, to divide by 10's or multiply by 10's is simply a matter of moving the decimal point to the right or to the left.

For example, 1 gram or liter or meter can be written:

1. To multiply or increase by 10 move the decimal point in this way:

    10. and so on
   100. (one hundred)
 1000. (one thousand)

2. To divide by 10 move the decimal in this way:

  1. (one)
 .1 (one-tenth)
 .01 (one-hundredth)
 .001 (one-thousandth)

14.

But, When?

Possibly by the time you read this Congress may have finally made the change to metrics official. Even so, it will be "voluntary," and it may take ten years before the system is used widely enough for the change to be considered accomplished.

One reason given by some Congressmen who voted against the metric bill in May, 1974, is the possibility that the government would be giving money to certain businesses and organizations to help pay for changing tools and equipment. There would also be the expense of changes in many government agencies. Some Congressmen feared the cost to the taxpayers would run into billions of dollars, as much as $60 billion.

Supporters of the metric bill stated that the cost would be $14 million over a five-year period. That money would be for the operation of a national conversion board to coordinate the voluntary conversion to metrics.

That the United States will officially adopt the metric system of measurements seems inevitable. Of course, it has seemed inevitable for most of the past hundred years.

Official or not, metric measurements will be used increasingly on the American scene. The U.S. Department of Agriculture may already be using standard global metric terms in its regular crop reports. It had planned to do so beginning May 8, 1974, which by coincidence was the day after the House of Representatives rejected the system, 240 to 153.

It may be confusing while metric is one of our many systems. But as use of metric measurement spreads, from voluntary and unofficial to the day it is voluntary and official, we all will benefit. True, there will be some disruption and expenses for businessmen and individuals. But in the long and short run, the benefits to all will be much greater than the temporary inconveniences.

Table of Equivalents

1 angstrom	0.000 000 1 millimeter 0.000 000 004 inch
1 cable length	219.456 meters 720 feet
1 centimeter	0.3937 inch
1 chain (Gunter's or surveyor's)	20.1168 meters 66 feet
1 decimeter	3.937 inches
1 dekameter	32.808 feet
1 fathom	1.8288 meters 6 feet
1 foot	0.3048 meter
1 furlong	201.168 meters 220 yards
1 inch	2.54 centimeters
1 kilometer	0.621 mile

1 league (land)	4.828 kilometers 3 statute miles
1 meter	39.37 inches
1 micron	0.001 millimeter 0.000 039 37 inch
1 mil	0.001 inch 0.025 4 millimeter
1 mile (land)	1.609 kilometer 5,280 feet
1 mile (nautical)	1.852 kilometers 1.151 statute miles
1 millimeter	0.039 37 inch
1 millimicron	0.001 micron 0.000 000 039 37 inch
1 point (type)	0.351 millimeter 0.013 837 inch
1 rod (pole or perch)	5.0292 meters 16½ feet
1 yard	0.9144 meter

AREAS

1 acre	0.405 hectare 43,560 square feet 4,840 square yards
1 are	0.025 acre 119.599 square yards
1 hectare	2,471 acres
1 square centimeter	0.155 square inch
1 square decimeter	15.500 square inches
1 square foot	929.030 square centimeters
1 square inch	6.4516 square centimeters
1 square kilometer	0.386 square mile
1 square meter	1.196 square yards
1 square mile	258.999 hectares
1 square millimeter	0.002 square inch
1 square rod	25.293 square meters
1 square yard	0.836 square meter

VOLUMES or CAPACITIES

1 barrel (liquid)*

1 barrel (fruits and vegetables except cranberries)	7,056 cubic inches 105 dry quarts
1 barrel (cranberry)	5,286 cubic inches
1 bushel (U.S. struck measure)	35.239 liters 2,150.42 cubic inches
1 bushel (U.S. heaped)	1,278 bushels (struck) 2,747.715 cubic inches
1 cord (firewood)	128 cubic feet
1 cubic centimeter	0.061 cubic inch
1 cubic decimeter	61.024 cubic inches
1 cubic foot	28.316 cubic decimeters 7.481 gallons
1 cubic inch	16.387 cubic centimeters

*Barrel is not an exact liquid measurement. The volume will vary greatly, according to the actual liquid the barrel is to contain.

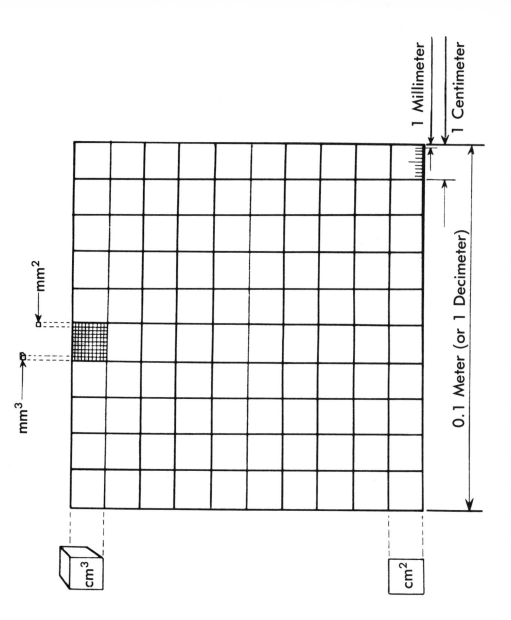

The centimeter squared and cubed, with the millimeter also squared and cubed.

1 cubic meter	1.308 cubic yards
1 cubic yard	0.765 cubic meter
1 cup (measuring)	8 fluid ounces
1 dram (U.S. fluid)	3.697 milliliters
1 dekaliter	2.642 gallons
1 gallon (U.S.)	3.785 liters
1 gallon (British)	4.546 liters
1 gill	0.118 liter
1 hectoliter	26.418 gallons
1 liter	1.057 liquid quarts 0.908 dry quart
1 milliliter	0.271 fluid dram 16.231 minims
1 ounce (U.S. liquid)	29.574 milliliters
1 peck	8.810 liters
1 pint (dry)	0.551 liter

1 pint (liquid)	0.473 liter
1 quart (dry U.S.)	1.101 liters
1 quart (liquid U.S.)	0.846 liter
1 tablespoon	3 teaspoons ½ fluid ounce
1 teaspoon	$^1/_3$ tablespoon

MASS (or WEIGHT)

1 carat	200 milligrams
1 dram (apothecary)	3.888 grams
1 dram (avoirdupois)	1.772 grams
1 grain	64.79891 milligrams
1 gram	15.432 grains
1 kilogram	2.205 pounds
1 microgram	0.000001 gram

1 milligram	0.015 grain
1 ounce (avoirdupois)	28.350 grams
1 ounce (troy)	31.103 grams
1 pennyweight	1.555 grams
1 point	2 milligrams 0.01 carat
1 pound (avoirdupois)	453.59237 grams
1 pound (troy)	373.242 grams
1 ton (gross or long)	1.016 metric tons
1 ton (metric)	0.984 gross ton
1 ton (net or short)	0.907 metric ton

A few examples of fractions to decimal to millimeter:

Fract.	Dec.	Mm.
1/64	.0156	.397
1/32	.03125	.794

Fract.	Dec.	Mm.
1/16	.0625	1.588
1/8	.1250	3.175
1/4	.2500	6.350
1/2	.500	12.700

INDEX

93

94

The Author

William Moore has been a teacher of industrial arts in New York City public schools and is currently an instructor in the Department of Industrial Education at the City University of New York. He is the author of *How Fast? How Far? How Much?*, a book on the various standards of measurements used in science, industry, and everyday life. Mr. Moore, who has become well known for his magazine articles in the field of woodwork, metalcraft, and how-to-do-its, is a graduate of Ohio State University. He and his family live in Brooklyn, New York.

DATE DUE